ALEXAND

A Life from Beginning To End

BY

HENRY FREEMAN

© 2016 Copyright

No part of this book may be reproduced in any form or by any electronic or mechanical means including information storage and retrieval systems, without permission in writing from the author.

Table of Contents

Alexander and the Happiness of Horses

Aristotle and the First Day of School

Philip's Family Drama

Enemies and Friends

The Real Battle Begins

Changing Tides

Signs and Wonders

In Pursuit of Darius

Historical Autopsy

Introduction
Alexander and the Happiness of Horses

Alexander, the son of the Macedonian King Philip II, was born in the year 356 BCE. The day that the King received word of Alexander's birth was a happy one indeed: as the story goes, on the day that Alexander was born, Philip was away on a military campaign when three messengers bearing good tidings simultaneously burst in upon his tent one after the other.

The first messenger told him the encouraging news that one of his generals had just managed to overthrow one of his worst enemies, the Illyrians. Shortly after this encouraging word, another messenger appeared and to the King's great pleasure notified him that, of all things, his favorite horse back home had just won a race in the Olympic Games. And then finally a third messenger rushed up to King Philip's tent to declare the birth of his son, Alexander.

From an early age Alexander was a beloved child, but this didn't mean that his parents were overprotective or especially doting. His father Philip made it clear from the beginning that he wanted his son to work hard and to achieve his right to his father's throne through hardship and abstinence from luxury. Aiding Philip in his desire to harden his son was the wizened old veteran of his court, Leonidas, who drilled Alexander like a soldier from the first day he could walk.

As early as two years old Alexander was instructed in the military arts of archery, swordplay, and horsemanship. And out of all of these martial practices, it was mounting a horse and tearing across the Macedonian countryside on a powerful steed that Alexander loved beyond anything else. It was this love of horses that would bring about one of the most powerful Alexandrian legends.

When Alexander was only 12 years old, a famous horse breeder from Thessaly arrived at his father's court wishing to sell his horses to the King. Being a man who loved a good thoroughbred just as much as his son, Philip jumped at the chance to acquire another good steed. Yet when the breeder introduced to them to his best horse, a beautiful black stallion called Bucephalas, its behavior left a lot to be desired despite the horse's majestic appearance.

Apparently the horse was a bit skittish and upon being approached it would rear up on its hind legs, neighing in fearful protest to anyone who attempted to ride him. Disgusted with the horse's feckless behavior, the annoyed King ordered the horse to be sent away. Yet even though his father had given up on the cantankerous horse, the young Alexander had not; he pleaded with Philip to allow him to try his own luck with Bucephalus before he sent it away.

Alexander, always being a shrewd interpreter of events as they unfolded, had noticed that the horse seemed the most afraid when the sun was casting the horse's shadow in front of it. Realizing that the horse was scared of its own shadow more than anything else, Alexander led the horse out of the sunlight until it no longer cast such a frightful shade. He then spent a few moments coaxing the horse, stroking its mane and talking to it gently until he thought it was relaxed enough that he could mount.

Alexander then led the horse slowly out in the grassland, keeping a careful grip on its reins. Once he had trotted the horse out into more open pasture, to the astonishment of the onlookers he let go of the reins completely and allowed the horse to take off like a bullet at full speed. The crowd was terrified and feared the worst, thinking that Alexander had lost control of the horse and would be killed or seriously injured by the wild beast.

Alexander had other plans though. To the joy of his father, the young prince returned a short time later with a much more docile horse under his command. Everyone present viewed Alexander's successful mastery of this wild horse as an important milestone for the young prince and a sure sign of his future greatness.

His father King Philip is said to have wept for joy, and declared, "My son, you must seek out a kingdom equal to yourself—Macedonia is not big enough for you!" So it was that yet another happy milestone was reached in the Macedonian kingdom, and the beginning of Alexander's coming of age was marked through the happiness of horses.

Chapter One

Aristotle and the First Day of School

As Alexander quickly matured and embarked upon adolescence, his father realized that he needed a skilled tutor to instruct his son not only in the physical arena, but also in the theatre of the mind. For King Philip only one man was worthy of this task: the Greek Philosopher and prolific writer, Aristotle.

A student of Plato at the famed Academy in Athens, Aristotle had planned on taking over leadership of the school when his mentor died. However instead of taking charge, after Plato's death Aristotle was sent fleeing for his life, ironically enough because of his connections to King Philip. Aristotle had known Philip since they were both children. Aristotle's father was actually the court physician for Philip's own father and from here Aristotle had developed strong ties to the Macedonian kingdom.

These strong bonds did not fare so well when a virulently anti-Macedonian wing of Athens took over the academy after Plato's demise. It was Aristotle's flight from the hostile political climate of Athens that led him right into his mentorship of the young Alexander. Always making a strong impression, what with his skinny legs, small eyes, stilted accent and flamboyant clothing, Aristotle could make Alexander laugh just as easily as he could produce thoughtful introspection.

Although at the time of Alexander's tutelage Aristotle had not yet composed his greatest works in philosophy, Aristotle was still a thought-provoking and far-reaching teacher nonetheless. He exhorted the young prince to immerse himself in studying logic, ethics, and even psychology. Yet despite Aristotle's heavy push for Alexander to acquaint himself with these civic lessons, the young Macedonian's favorite subject was always that of the epic poet Homer and his lore of daring heroes and great warriors.

The young Alexander, seeing a template for his own future exploits in the likes of Odysseus and Achilles, couldn't get enough of this mythology. Although Aristotle would have preferred his student focus on subjects of government administration rather than epic tales of conquest, he didn't discourage this interest, even going as far as to having a special copy of Homer's work prepared for his student.

This was no small feat in the days prior to the printing press since all books had to be laboriously copied by hand. Alexander appreciated it however, and it quickly became his most prized possession. In fact, it is said that in one famous instance, when Alexander came across the crown jewels of Persia, he dumped out the Persian king's most prized possessions and filled the box with his own in turn, depositing his copy of the Homeric epic into the box!

However, until that day Alexander would carry this text of epic poetry and heroic legend with him in all of his battles, protected in a golden box. Alexander was a man who wanted to carry his passion with him wherever he went. This passion would serve him well when the anti-Macedonian uprising in Athens that had turned his teacher Aristotle into a refugee congealed into an all-out war.

As the political situation turned from bad to worse, King Philip sought to launch a preemptive strike against the troubling city-state by seizing their grain shipments and then capturing the nearby Greek city of Elatea. Philip hoped that by these bold strikes against Athenian interests he could provoke Athens into an attack. Philip's wish was soon granted as the enraged Athenians whipped their populace into a frenzy and launched an immediate offensive against the Macedonians.

It was in the withering heat of August 338 BCE that the Athenian army began their showdown with the army of King Philip in a narrow valley in central Greece. Both armies were said to be fairly evenly matched with about 60,000 men on each side, rushing at each other headlong. It was in the middle of this intense, pitched battle that King Philip would give his then 18 year old son Alexander the chance to prove his mettle as a military leader, giving him command of an entire wing of the army.

It was also Alexander who faced the stiffest resistance of the onslaught; the crack unit of fighters, known as the "Sacred Band of Thebes", stood their ground and faced off against Alexander's cavalry until every man among them was either dead or severely wounded, even as the rest of Athenian army broke ranks. King Philip was so inspired by their bravery that he commissioned a giant lion to be built on the spot to memorialize the valor of his vanquished foes.

Philip proved to be fairly magnanimous in victory, and even though some had advised him to move in on Athens and finish the job, the king refused to march on the city. Instead he sent out a delegation led by Alexander to the Athenian assembly in order to hammer out a peace treaty. Generosity aside, this was also a very pragmatic move on the King's part since he understood the power of the Athenian navy, and he wagered that it would be much more to his advantage if he could acquire that great sea power through peace rather than risk destroying it through force.

This decisive move towards diplomacy seemed to work perfectly in the king's favor, and the anxious Athenians were so thankful not to have to face Macedonian troops at their doorstep that they were ready to offer Philip anything he wanted. After the peace deal was struck the Athenians immediately granted both King Philip and Alexander with citizenship and even put a statue of Philip in their marketplace to show their gratitude to the Macedonian king.

For Alexander, entrance into the grand city he had heard so many stories about from his instructor Aristotle was an amazing adventure. He saw the Acropolis and marveled at the Parthenon and other famous Greek sites as he received his first real taste of Hellenistic civilization. He even took a tour of the Academy where his teacher had taught before fleeing the city, taking in all of the treasures of the land whose ideals he would later espouse. Suddenly all of Aristotle's teachings seemed more like just a prelude; for Alexander this was the true first day of school.

Chapter Two
Philip's Family Drama

It was in the aftermath of some of Philip's most stunning successes that one of the strangest and most unpredictable dramas began to unfold. As soon as Philip returned to the Macedonian capital of Pella he declared that he was going to divorce his longtime wife, Alexander's mother Olympias, on grounds of adultery. Much worse than this, Philip began to spread rumors of his uncertainty over whether or not Alexander was even his son. You can imagine how much of a slap in the face this must have felt to Alexander who had just served his father so well in battle, only to have his own father practically disown him shortly afterwards.

It soon became clear however that these bizarre charges were rooted in the fact that his father desired a new wife. This new target of his heart's desires also bore the promise of a purer Macedonian bloodline. Philip had always been a bit anxious over Alexander's mother's foreign background (she was from the mountainous region of Epirus), so he jumped at the opportunity to produce an heir of purer Macedonian stock. His new bride was the niece of one of his generals, a man named Attalus, whose lineage offered a much more noble background for the Macedonian Kingdom than the backwaters of Epirus ever could.

However, soon after putting Olympias and Alexander in effective exile, Philip began to feel sorry for his son. In an ill-conceived attempt to smooth over relations with his son, he invited him to attend his wedding banquet. Alexander grudgingly attended; amidst the tension, wine was soon flowing heavily through the banquet hall. All of the guests were fairly intoxicated when General Attalus raised his glass to give a toast to his niece and King Philip.

It was then that Attalus, either in complete drunken stupidity or flat out disregard for Alexander, declared that all Macedonians should pray for the gods to grant Philip and his new bride a "legitimate successor to the throne." Alexander, who until very recently was the unquestioned heir apparent, was understandably furious, leaping out of his seat to hurl his cup at Attalus and asking the general if was calling him a bastard.

In the chaos that ensued, Philip leapt to his feet. However, instead of defending his son, he drew his sword and stepped toward Alexander as if he was going to cut him down. In his drunken stupor, all he managed to accomplish was to trip and fall flat on his face. The still highly infuriated Alexander was then left to stand over his father and proclaim to all the party goers in venomous sarcasm, "Look everyone! The man who wants to cross Europe to Asia can't even make it from one couch to the next."

Alexander, realizing there was nothing left for him in his father's kingdom, then made a quick exit and fled back to his mother's family home in the mountains of Epirus. Several months went by with Philip and Alexander remaining in cold silence. Meanwhile, Philip and his new bride were vigorously attempting to create a new heir to the throne, with his first efforts producing a daughter, Europa, several months later.

After disowning Alexander, Philip was still without a male heir. With prospects of war with the Persian Empire looming on the horizon, many began to feel very unsettled about the contentious political landscape. Realizing how precarious things were becoming, King Philip finally came to his senses and decided to reestablish Alexander as his rightful heir before it was too late.

Philip then sent messengers out to find his son and bring him back to the kingdom. Alexander returned, still embittered from his previous experience, and soon became full of his own plots and intrigues against the kingdom. Keeping his ear to the ground, he soon discovered that his father was attempting to marry his sister off to Alexander's own uncle back in Epirus. This was apparently another attempt to sooth the frayed relationship the Macedonian kingdom had suffered with the region after Philip's divorce.

In order to celebrate this wedding, Philip called for another grand celebration, this time in the town of Vergina, a major heartland of Macedonia and a place that was known as the official burial grounds of kings. The festivities seemed to top even those of Philip's own recent wedding, and included everything from extravagant banquets to even live athletic games for entertainment.

The guest list was packed with many notables, but the behavior of two of these distinguished guests would serve as omens for the tragedy to come. The first event occurred when the Athenian ambassador who presented King Philip with a golden crown proclaimed that anyone who dared plot against the king would be hunted down by the people of Athens. Then, seconding this ominous portent in an even more shocking way was the famed entertainer Neoptolemus who sang a song for the king with the lyrics, "Your dreams soar higher than the sky, of greater fields to sow, of palaces grander then men have ever known. But death is coming, sudden, unseen, that robs us of our distant hopes."

At the time many perceived these song lyrics to be a challenge to the Persian king, projecting his coming demise at the hands of Philip, but soon after their utterance these words proved to be a prophesy of a whole other order - one viciously played out when in the middle of the wedding ceremony, one of the king's own bodyguards reached in his cloak, pulled out a dagger, and plunged it into King Philip's heart. The murderer's name was Pausanias, and he was certainly no stranger to King Philip; in fact, this man had once been the king's lover.

It was no secret that King Philip had many affairs with young men throughout his life, and the culture of ancient Greece had no qualms with such relationships. The drama came however when Philip grew tired of Pausanias and turned his favors toward another young man. His former lover couldn't quite get over this rejection and soon began a vigorous slander campaign against the other young man, spreading vicious rumors, and charging that he was, among other things, an effeminate coward.

Philip's new lover, apparently being fairly sensitive about his reputation, sought to disprove these charges by purposefully throwing himself on the frontlines in battle, an effort that ultimately cost him his life. This unfortunate young man happened to be the best friend of General Attalus, the same General whose niece Philip would later marry. As the story goes, when this general heard of his friend's demise due to the taunts and bullying of Pausanias, Attalus crafted a plan of revenge and invited him over for a drink.

The unsuspecting Pausanias obliged the invitation and apparently, after being plied with much food and wine, the young man passed out. It was then that the account takes on a horribly vicious tone, indicating that the passed out Pausanias was repeatedly gang raped by Attalus and the other dinner guests. Humiliated, Pausanias sought justice for this egregious transgression from the king.

Philip for his part was said to be completely horrified by what Attalus did, but was hesitant to punish the general since he needed his military prowess and political connections in order for his Persian invasion to be successful. With no recourse for what had happened to him, Pausanias's rage and rejection reached a boiling point; and it was for this obvious injustice that he killed King Philip.

If the stories revolving around Philip and Pausanias are true it would certainly give Pausanias more than enough motive to commit the act, but as it stands, we may never really know since Pausanias was himself cut down immediately after stabbing the king. The revenge of a spurned and obviously mistreated lover is a good explanation, but even without it, there was more than enough drama in the king's family to point fingers elsewhere.

Over the millennia, there have been countless other theories in the impetus behind the assassination. Philip not only had a spurned lover to deal with; he also had a spurned son and wife, and many have pointed their fingers at Olympias and Alexander as being the true culprits, projecting the theory that Pausanias was just the hired assassin that they had lined up for the deed. Whatever the case may be, it was Philip's family drama that led to Alexander becoming king.

Chapter Three

Enemies and Friends

After his father's death, it was Alexander's number one priority to consolidate his claim to the throne and find as many allies as he could who would be sympathetic to his bid for power. Immediately after his father's untimely demise, Alexander was facing a kingdom that was truly torn asunder. Most of the other heads of state in the Greek neighborhood viewed the young Macedonian as, in the words of the infamous Greek orator and rabble rouser Demosthenes, as nothing more than a "young fool playing the king on his father's throne."

In this chaotic climate one would think that perhaps the young king would focus all of his efforts on internal affairs and attempt to put off any exterior conflict for a later date. Yet Alexander surprised everyone during this tumult by immediately setting his army marching to the south to take on the contentious army of Thessaly; the Thessalian force was blocking the road to Mount Olympus, bringing the further advance of the Macedonian military to a halt, and Alexander was determined to stop it.

Alexander knew that it would be a suicidal charge if he sent his men out in a direct assault. No doubt taking some of Aristotle's lessons in logic to heart, Alexander reasoned that if he couldn't go through the garrison at Thessaly, then he would go around it. To do this, Alexander quickly commissioned a unit of engineers to build an alternative path on the far side of Mount Ossa.

Due to this unexpected stroke of genius, the forces of Thessaly were caught completely off guard and before they could even process what was happening they were completely outflanked. Faced with certain death if they resisted, the Thessalians quickly capitulated and agreed to recognize Alexander as the heir to Phillip, paying homage and taxes to the king; of the most immediate, strategic importance, they agreed to turn over their crack unit of cavalry to Alexander as a special auxiliary to his army.

It was that in this masterful stroke of military strategy and political diplomacy that Alexander managed to solidify Thessaly and enable a much needed enhancement to his military might. He then continued his campaign southward to the Greek cities of Thermopylae and Thebes. Of these two the Thebans were the most rebellious group, as they had greatly resented the reign of Philip—let alone his fresh faced son—and were at the moment indisposed to capitulate to the young man's demands.

However, despite this long antagonism, Alexander had impressed them so much with the speed in which he managed to bring his full force to bear right outside their gates that the Thebans soon realized that they had greatly underestimated the new king. And so once again, just like in Thessaly, the city of Thebes surrendered without a fight. Hearing of how easily their Theban neighbors had capitulated, the Athenians then immediately sent an envoy out to Alexander to broker a peace deal.

They weren't disappointed, as Alexander desired cooperation more than conquest and sent them back a generous peace treaty. King Alexander then marched his men past Athens and on into Corinth where he met with the Corinthian League; knowing they were beat, just like so many of their other Greek counterparts, the League declared Alexander "leader for life" and pledged their full support.

It was in this moment that Alexander showed the truly mischievous side of his genius. He produced an actor before the Corinthians whom he had paid to pretend he was a refugee from the Eastern Greek city of Ephesus. This actor was apparently rather convincing and, laying it on as thick as he could, proceeded to plead with the representatives to help Alexander free his oppressed city from the tyrannical abuses of the Persian king.

If this actor was alive today he probably would have won an Academy Award. The Corinthian delegation was powerfully moved by his story and rose to applaud and cheer, crying out their undying support to overthrow the unjust Persians. They then nominated Alexander as the general to lead the new Pan-Hellenic League to war against Persia. Whether through sheer force of will, political intrigue or outright deception, Alexander knew very well the importance of making coalitions.

Yet he also learned that friends and allies could be very fickle. As soon as Alexander was about to cross the border into Persia, he began to receive word of rebellions sparking against him all throughout the Hellenic world. Chief among these rebellions was an insurrection of a group of fierce Illyrian tribes led by Cleitus, an old enemy of Alexander's father, and King Glaucias of the Tauntalians.

When Alexander turned back to face this threat, from the very beginning he was greatly outnumbered. However, Alexander was ready, determined to subdue his enemy with weapons of mass distraction. To the bewilderment of his enemy he had his soldiers, who had been routinely drilled in their maneuvers, march out in front of their opponents and put on a kind of military parade. The curious enemy couldn't help but watch in fascination as Alexander's men raised their spears in perfect unison, marching to the left and then marching to the right, as the entire unit pinwheeled like one living machine in organized patterns across the field before them, all in complete silence.

After thoroughly mesmerizing and bewildering their enemy in this fashion, Alexander then suddenly gave the signal for attack; once again, his men, in complete synchronization, ferociously beat their spears to their shields. They finally broke their prolonged silence, and with a battle cry that scared their opponents to death, charged the enemy. With Alexander's forces employing a brilliant piece of psychological warfare, the Illyrians were sent running for the hills.

It wasn't long after the Illyrian defeat that another Greek polis would soon be waging rebellion. And this time the discontent was being stirred up by a very old thorn in the side of the Macedonian Kingdom. The great orator Disonenes, who had cowered in fear during the previous capitulation of Athens, had regained some of his nerve in Alexander's absence and had been busy rallying the Athenians towards rebellion.

One of his chief arguments for the revolt was actually that Alexander was dead. No one had seen the young king in months, and many wondered if he may very well have perished in one of his campaigns, and so it was that Disonenes made sure that it was his job to spread this rumor as much as he could. Perhaps taking a page out of Alexander's own playbook, he even managed to procure an actor and have him show up at the town council wrapped in bandages, appearing to be badly beaten and bruised. This actor then proclaimed what the rumor mills had already been peddling, and declared to everyone that he witnessed Alexander die in battle.

No city received this false rumor of Alexander's demise happier than the city of Thebes. After receiving their perceived good tidings, the Thebans ambushed a Macedonian garrison stationed outside of their city. The ambushers then went to the Theban assembly and bragged about their deeds, issuing a challenge to everyone assembled and declaring that all of Thebes should join their fight in overthrowing the Macedonians.

The reaction was immediate. The Thebans enthusiastically agreed and rushed headlong toward the Macedonian fortress known as the "Cadmeia". They quickly dug trenches and built palisades in order to deny the Macedonian defenders of supplies and reinforcements. But the supposedly dead Alexander had a swift response as well; as soon as he received notification of this uprising, he sent his army racing toward Thebes to shut the rebellion down.

After his arrival, the Thebans, seeking to gain some friends loyal to their cause, mounted the towers of their city walls and called out to Alexander's men that anyone who wished to desert the tyranny of his rule was welcome among them. Not only that, when Alexander tried to declare that he was bringing peace to the Greeks, the Thebans manning the towers rebuked him by obstinately declaring the Persians as their true liberators and then further exhorted Alexander's men to join them.

According to the chroniclers of this event, there was something about being called a tyrant, coupled with the Thebans invoking the great enemy upon whom he had been set to engage in battle before their rebellion, that caused Alexander to snap. It was bad enough that the city of Thebes had already been a troublesome thorn in both he and his father's side for the past 30 years, but now the citizens were directly denouncing him to his face as a tyrannical leader while at the same time embracing his sworn enemy. This was just too much for him to deal with. Alexander now found himself completely enraged by this belligerent city; the incredible anger that they had stoked inside of him would spell the doom of Thebes.

The Thebans put up a fierce resistance but in the end they were no match for Alexander's army. Within hours, the city had been taken. The death toll for Thebes is said to have been 6000, while 30,000 more were taken prisoner. Of these 30,000, most were sold into slavery. As a product of Alexander's wrath, since they had refused to join them of their own free will, he consigned the whole rebellious lot to a life of slavery. Seeking to wipe Thebes completely off the map, he then set the proud Greek city on fire. As Alexander watched the former stronghold of his opponents turn to ash, he drew a firm line in the sand between his enemies and his friends.

Chapter Four
The Real Battle Begins

It was in 334 BCE that Alexander would launch his armies on a mission of conquest against the Persian Empire. He had his men press eastward over vast marches where they then followed the Hebros River on down to the Gallipoli Peninsula. Even though there was a large Persian fleet active along the coasts of the Aegean, Alexander's army managed to slip by them without any incident. It is said that even before Alexander leapt ashore he threw his spear from his vessel, plunging it into the beach in declaration of his conquest.

Alexander and his men then continued their march on foot where they were virtually unopposed. It wasn't until they left the Persian controlled but still very much Greek city of Priapus that they would finally encounter the enemy, camped out some 20 miles away across the Granicus River near the Persian town of Zeleia. Alexander's first clear picture of what he was facing came to him in the form of his scouts who relayed back to him that the Persians had a massive cavalry in formation on the far bank of the river.

According to the chroniclers who documented this event, despite advice from his commanders to delay his attack Alexander insisted that they strike the Persian force as quickly as possible while they still had the element of surprise. Facing off against thousands of Persian cavalry and infantry, Alexander directed his men in a standard battle formation with his own infantry in the center flanked by his cavalry on the sides, and then readied them to cross the river and charge the enemy.

At first there was a literal standoff as the Persians and Macedonians stood their ground, staring at each other across the river banks and with neither one making a definitive move. It was Alexander himself that ushered in the battle, by suddenly charging his horse across the river. A cacophony of trumpets and battle cries on both sides immediately followed to signify without a doubt that the battle had begun.

In the initial onslaught the Persian archers let loose with an intense volley of arrows, many of these aimed at Alexander who was unmistakable in his brightly shining, ornate armor. While many of his forces would suffer the sting of these arrows, Alexander was too fast for them, expertly guiding his horse Bucephalus through the torrent of arrows and directly to the front lines of the enemy.

It seems that one of the Persians' main strategies to deal with Alexander was just to kill him outright and end the battle early by taking its leader. For the rest of the battle, there was a concerted effort to isolate Alexander and take his life, with wave after wave of Persian fighters charging his position. However, Alexander's men rallied around him and worked feverishly to drive the Persians back.

Alexander faced death several times, in one instance while he was fighting a Persian nobleman in front of him. The young Macedonian king was dealt a ferocious blow to the back of his head by a Persian fighter on horseback. Alexander's helmet saved his life but the impact of his assailant's sword was so ferocious that it cleaved the helmet right in two, leaving Alexander's head unprotected for the rest of the battle.

Alexander faced death again only moments later when he was charged from behind by yet another round of Persian cavalry. He was saved when one of his commanders selflessly threw himself at the Persian warrior, cutting the attacker's arm off, leaving the now mortally wounded Persian's arm and sword to fall to the bloodstained ground below. At this point about a thousand Persian horsemen had been cut down. The Persians realized that their chance of winning the battle had vanished, so the battered army began to make a slow retreat.

After the battle was over, Alexander took the time to bury the dead and to also take a few spoils of war. Among these he gathered up about 300 pieces of armor off of the dead Persian soldiers and, intending to ship these spoils of war back to Greece, had a very striking message inscribed on their surface: "Alexander son of Philip and all the Greeks—Except the Spartans—sent these spoils from the Barbarians of Asia". Showing a bit of his humor and irony, Alexander set the record straight about just who was supporting him.

Many more cities would fall before the Macedonians, many of them without a fight - as was the case with the "battle" for the city of Sardis, in which the Persian commander met Alexander's forces outside the city walls and immediately offered to surrender. It is a bit unclear what the commander's motives were, as he had the numbers and the supplies to hold off Alexander's men long enough for more Persian reinforcements to arrive, but at any rate, a relieved Alexander accepted his bid for peace.

Sardis proved to be a city full of riches. The gold stores of the town provided a much needed boost of morale to Alexander and his soldiers. After acquiring these resources, Alexander could for the first time pay his army for their services while also replenishing his own much depleted coffers. After everything was squared away in Sardis, Alexander then marched his army on a four day journey to the neighboring coastal city of Ephesus, a town which had been founded hundreds of years before by Greeks but had long since fallen under Persian dominion.

The Ephesians had previously supported Alexander's father Philip, and here once again Alexander found support for himself as well. However, the Ephesians were now split in their sentiment, a brief civil war of sorts springing up between the democrats who pledged loyalty to Alexander and the aristocratic minority that supported Persia. The Greek loyalists prevailed however and the Persian-supporting aristocracy of Ephesus was put out of business.

Once Ephesus was firmly under his control, Alexander launched a kind of military parade to celebrate his diplomatic triumph and to display his military capabilities. Neighboring towns soon took notice and then sent their own envoys to pledge their allegiance to Alexander. As the Macedonian king marched through Asia Minor, cities seemed ready to capitulate just upon seeing his army. However, one town in his path would change their minds.

The city of Miletus, a strategic naval location, wanted to offer Alexander their surrender, but when they realized a fleet of Persian ships were nearby they thought otherwise, rescinding their offer and barring their gates against the Macedonian army. Alexander immediately ordered his own Greek navy to converge on the harbor so the Persian ships could not get through, forcing the Persians to set anchor 10 miles off course.

Alexander then set his corps of engineers to work, having them tear a hole through the city walls of Miletus, in which they succeeded beyond expectation, creating such a massive opening that the entire Macedonian army could charge through. Alexander then prepared his men for a Persian invasion from the enemy fleet, but this invasion force never came; the Macedonians gained an unchallenged foothold in the region with the Persians simply reduced to occasionally attacking Alexander from the sea.

It was at this point that Alexander made the unexpected move of disbanding his own navy. Historians have vigorously debated the reasoning behind this, but it seems that at this point Alexander realized that his small fleet would be insignificant against the massive Persian naval force and decided it would be better to put all of his energy behind a strike over land rather than risk losses at sea.

This in turn greatly expanded the scope of Alexander's plans for conquest, since the only way he could shut down the Persian fleet by land was to deny them safe harbor on the coasts. This meant that Alexander would have to capture every port city along the Eastern Mediterranean. His first major challenge in this task would come in the form of the port city of Halicarnassus. The Persian fleet was out of reach, safely moored within the city's harbors, and the city itself was completely encircled in heavy walls. Meanwhile the Persian General Menmom, who had taken over the city, was able to send out battalions of his troops at will, bursting them through the city gates at irregular intervals to keep Alexander's men completely off balance.

Making things even more difficult, the Persians had dug formidable trenches around the city walls. These trenches had to be filled if the Macedonians were ever going to be able to break through to the city, but even approaching the trenches became a lethal hazard as Alexander's men were brutally shot down by Persian archers stationed from watchtowers. Knowing that his men didn't stand a chance unless they had some sort of protection, he devised a plan for groups of soldiers to shelter themselves under movable sheds as they approached, but even this wasn't enough to protect them from the Persian rain of death.

Alexander seethed in frustration as arrows and giant boulders crushed his best soldiers and engineers, but the city walls wouldn't budge. The siege then carried on through the summer and into the fall, with intermittent skirmishes claiming lives on both sides. The Macedonians however fared the better in these battles and the death toll was always slightly better on their end.

As autumn began to turn to winter, with supplies and manpower finally dwindling, Menmom and his men made a hasty exit, finally leaving the city to Alexander in a long awaited battle won mostly through attrition. It was a victory nonetheless, and now Alexander was one major step closer to his goal of controlling the entire Aegean coast of Asia Minor.

Alexander would then spend the rest of that winter moving further inland and consolidating his gains, with most of the towns he encountered offering immediate surrender. Things seemed to be going very well for the Macedonian conquest, but while Alexander was busy subduing all of Asia Minor, General Menmom decided to take the fight straight to Macedonia itself. After occupying the strategic islands of Chios and Lesbos, he made overtures to disgruntled Spartans and Athenians declaring that if they sided with him he would overthrow their Macedonian overlords.

To the horror of Alexander most of the Greeks met this news with unbridled enthusiasm, leaving the Macedonian King betrayed on the home front once again. This created a horrible dilemma for Alexander: if he dropped everything and ran back to Macedonia to stave off a Persian invasion he would lose everything he had gained in Asia Minor, and yet if he stayed away he risked losing the very heart of his kingdom.

Chapter Five
Changing Tides

When Alexander heard that the Menmon was poised to invade his homeland of Macedonia with the full backing of many of the Greek city-states, the outlook for Alexander couldn't have been worse. Yet fate, or "the gods" as Alexander probably believed, were smiling upon him on that day. By sheer chance, right before Menmon was to undertake the invasion, he fell ill and died.

This struck a severe blow to any plans of invasion. His successor was inexperienced and unlike Menmon virtually unknown among the Greeks, causing them to become unsure of themselves and back out of their plans of treachery altogether. This was a definitive stroke of good luck for Alexander, and with the Persian invasion of Macedonia scrapped he was now free to finalize his conquest in the East.

Ironically enough, while subduing villages and city-states all throughout the region, Alexander almost singlehandedly ruined the whole expedition. It wasn't military defeat that ground the Macedonian military machine to a halt but Alexander's own youthful ignorance. Unexpected calamity occurred when Alexander, who was suffering from heat exhaustion, thought it would be a good idea to take a dive in the cool rivers of Tarsus.

His army had been marching for days in the staggering heat of the Cilician plains when they reached the city. Upon seeing the cool rivers that ran along its outskirts, Alexander ripped off his clothes and jumped right into water. Despite the scorching heat outside, the source of this river was from the frigid mountains; to the surprise of Alexander, the water was ice cold.

The unexpected frigidness of the water sent Alexander into shock, and as the blood drained from his face he found that he could no longer move his limbs. He began to sink to the bottom of the river bed. His soldiers immediately rushed forward and carried him out of the water before he was swept away by the icy currents. The quick action of his men saved him from sudden death, but as he lay in his tent on the outskirts of Tarsus, Alexander's condition went from bad to worse as he spent the next few days with a dangerously high fever, just barely clinging to life.

This was certainly a strange turn of events for the conquering Macedonian hero who had come to be known as Alexander the Great. As a consequence to this drama his army was thrown into a terrible panic, wondering what tragic fate would befall them if Alexander passed away and left them all stuck deep behind enemy lines with no one to lead them. It was in a state of both compassion for their king and terror for their own fate that his men patiently waited outside of his tent for him to recover.

Alexander had been languishing between life and death when his personal physician proposed to give him a special concoction that, allegedly, would stimulate his body and reverse the effects of the cold. Special potions and tonics were the standard treatment of the day, as Greek medicine of that time usually focused on maintaining a balance in the body. If the body was too cold, a concoction of hot peppers was administered, and if the body was too warm, healing oils were applied.

Not much of this ancient Greek alchemy can be said to be rooted in sound science, but whatever it was that his physician actually gave him, it seemed to do the trick. Perhaps the power of suggestion is more powerful than anything else, but as it stands, just a few hours after Alexander partook of this treatment his fever broke and he began to quickly regain his strength. Three days later he walked out of his tent, completely healed, to the roaring cheers of his Macedonian army.

Once his health was restored, Alexander tightened his grip on Tarsus and even took over the city's imperial Persian Mint, having the engravers issue out new coins with the image of Zeus and the name Alexander emblazoned on the surface. This clever propaganda tool Alexander used in order to make his legitimacy appear to grow in the region. It was also a humiliating embarrassment to the Persian Emperor Darius, who redoubled his efforts to stop the troublesome Macedonians, soon deciding to send out his entire army to finally deal a decisive death blow to Alexander's advance.

However, Darius delayed advancing on Alexander's position, preferring to stay in the open plains just north of the future city of Antioch. In doing so, Darius hoped he could somehow lure Alexander out in the open so that he could unleash the full might of his infantry and chariots. But Alexander, instead of coming right out in the open, remained among the mountain passes just out of the Persians' reach.

Losing his patience, Darius finally decided to forfeit his superior position in the plains to pursue the Macedonians in the mountains. It was here that confusion seemed to reign, as Darius, relying on faulty intelligence, actually wound up squeezed right behind the bulk of Alexander's advancing military into a tiny strip of land in between the mountains and the sea.

Alexander immediately recognized the great advantage he had been given, as the Persians, who carried larger numbers, were now forced to practically fight him single file in a narrow mountain pass. The Macedonians quickly did an about face and began the attack, throwing thousands of his infantry, flanked by Macedonian cavalry, at the mighty armies of the Persian Empire.

It is said that when Alexander led his men on the final charge against the Persians that they traveled at such a speed that they actually flew underneath the oncoming Persian arrows, arriving faster than the Persian archers could even take aim. Hitting the enemy at a full gallop, the Macedonians managed to break through the Persian battle formation, striking absolute terror in the front line troops.

The Persian defenses were on the verge of collapse when it was Darius's own Greek mercenaries who came to the rescue. Fighting desperately against the Macedonian infantry's center, they managed to cut through Alexander's main lines, tearing a gap in the Macedonian army's defenses. It is said that the ferociousness of these Greek mercenaries was able to drive Alexander's men back, killing many in the process while torrents of Greek insults were hurled back and forth on both sides.

Yet no matter the artfulness of the Greek mercenaries and their profanity, it was military strategy that won the day. Alexander managed to direct his forces to slowly encircle the mercenaries, forcing them to retreat. The Persian center then quickly began to fall apart; with their infantry lines crumbling, the whole Persian army was soon in full retreat with a panicked cavalry riding over the bodies of their own dead soldiers in order to escape.

Emperor Darius couldn't believe what was happening. He knew that the battle was lost, yet he would not surrender. He stood his ground while his own army was fleeing, standing boldly atop his chariot striking down anyone who approached. Alexander knew of course that the tide of battle had changed decisively in his favor; unable to resist the opportunity to strike this belligerent king down once and for all, he rushed headlong to meet Darius in battle.

A few of Darius's remaining cavalry saw this and attempted to come to their besieged leader's aid. However, Alexander managed to cut through them all and met Darius head on. The brief skirmish that ensued resulted in Darius wounding Alexander in the thigh before escaping with the rest of his retreating army. Alexander was elated with his victory but ultimately disappointed that he was so close to striking Darius down himself only to have him slip from his grasp.

Chapter Six
Signs and Wonders

With Darius on the run, Alexander sought to expand his holdings on the Eastern Mediterranean coast. This led him to capture the city of Tyre and then ultimately on to Jerusalem, where he demanded that the residents offer up supplies and a residual force of soldiers to incorporate into his army. However, initially, the Judean opinion was dead set against Alexander and they declared their allegiance to Persia.

Alexander was enraged at this rejection and determined to march on Jerusalem. However, right when Alexander arrived at the city gates, the high priest of the city, followed by a procession of wives and children, met him in order to quell his anger and demonstrate their peaceful intentions. Alexander was apparently impressed by the procession and jumped off his horse to meet them himself on foot to meet face-to-face with the high priest; peace was soon established.

After quelling discontent in Jerusalem, Alexander continued his mission of conquest and capitulation until he found his way to the city of Gaza, just south of modern day Israel. It was here that Alexander was once again beset with fierce resistance; due to the fact that the walls of Gaza rested on a high plain over the desert, mounting them appeared to be an insurmountable task.

Even so, Alexander set his engineers to work day and night to build great mounds up against the plain. Once these mounds were in place, Alexander's men used them to finally scale the walls and take the city. Once Gaza had been thoroughly subdued, Alexander then finally made his way to the land of his boyhood dreams: Egypt. Here he met a public opinion that was largely indifferent to his presence.

Egypt had lost its own national sovereignty years ago and even in Alexander's time, the days of the mighty Pharaohs were long behind them. For the most part the Egyptians didn't view Alexander with any more ire than they did the Persians or any other potential conqueror. However, Alexander was not quite like the rest; as his decisive victories began to stack up before him, he began to have his own delusions of grandeur.

It is said that at this point in his life that Alexander began to question whether or not King Philip was his father; he began to wonder instead whether he might actually be the son of a god. All of this sounds patently absurd to most of us today, but it was a common claim of many ancient kings of the past to assert that at least part of their parentage came from the heavens.

This inborn belief Alexander had was also further strengthened by his own childhood experiences. On the one hand he had his father who, at various times in his life, disowned him and outright denied that Alexander was his son; on the other hand, he had his mother who spread bizarre claims that she had been consumed by some sort of lightning bolt that shot through her bedroom window which somehow facilitated Alexander's conception.

With such wild speculations coming from his own parents it is little wonder that Alexander began to accept that the events of his birth were attached to something otherworldly. He sought to clarify this fact in Egypt by visiting a famous oracle 300 miles west of the Nile River in the middle of the Sahara. This was a religious site that was well known to the Greek world; there were all kinds of legends circulating around the location with stories of characters as famous as Hercules and Perseus making pilgrimages to the holy site.

So it was that Alexander, knee deep in the middle of enemy territory, risked life and limb to visit this holy place as well. It was here that he thought he finally found the answer to whether or not he was of divine parentage: as the story goes, when he met the priest of the shrine he was greeted with the words, "O' Paidon".

This was a traditional greeting used to any pilgrim, translated roughly as "Oh My Child," but for some reason this priest had a bad lisp that day and mispronounced his proclamation. Instead, what Alexander hard was "O' Pai Dios," which to his ears translated to "Oh Child of God".

Alexander, as superstitious as ever, took this as a clear sign that once and for all proved that he was without a doubt the son of a god. However, divine hubris, signs, and wonders aside, Alexander still had work to do; immediately after this proclamation, he began to make plans for his march on Mesopotamia.

Chapter Seven
In Pursuit of Darius

In his march through Mesopotamia, Alexander arrived at the banks of the Tigris in mid-September. At this point in time, his foe, the Persian Emperor Darius, had assembled a massive army, gathering troops from all corners of his empire in hot pursuit of Alexander's Macedonians. In fact, four days after crossing the Tigris, Alexander's advance cavalry was able to spot the Persian forces before them.

This first contingent of the Persian military force was an advance guard, comprised of around a thousand troops. Upon hearing this, Alexander ordered an immediate pursuit; upon catching up with the smaller force of Persian fighters, the Macedonians were able to cut them down without much of a loss to their own army.

From the few men that were left alive long enough to be captured Alexander, had learned that the main wing of Darius' army was stationed close by at the foothills of Nineveh, ready to strike Alexander in the open plains of the countryside. Apparently hoping to grant his men the advantage that they had been denied in their previous engagement, Darius was determined to fight Alexander out in the open. This time, Alexander could not refuse his request.

The next day, Alexander finally engaged Darius in battle. The Persian army stretched for miles across the plain in two broad lines, with the cavalry in front and the infantry behind. The center of Darius' formation was the most terrifying of all, with the huge multi-national infantry flanked by elephants from India and fearsome squadrons of chariots.

This seemingly unbeatable formation would strike terror in any other commander, but Alexander had other plans in mind. He realized that he would never be able to confront the vast bulk of the overwhelming Persian force directly, as they would quickly become encircled and destroyed. Instead he devised a diversionary tactic by pitting his entire legion to the right flank of Darius' army. Alexander then hoped that Darius would open up the center of his battle line in order to pursue the Macedonians.

Alexander believed this would create a major gap in the enemy lines, allowing them the opportunity to turn back around and engage the Persians directly through this strategic hole in their defenses. It was a daring plan, and one with a very slim chance of success, but Alexander was determined to make it work; as soon as the battle began, Alexander directed his men to engage in exactly the way that he had envisioned, sending the vast bulk of his forces to the right flank of the Persian army.

Darius walked right into Alexander's trap, breaking his battle lines just to pursue Alexander's madly dashing contingent. Once his ruse had been successful, Alexander cartwheeled his forces back to the middle of the Persian army, determined to strike right at the heart of his enemy, to finally take out Darius, and to deal the Persians a devastating blow. Alexander and his immediate circle fought vigorously through the Persian swords and spears to reach King Darius, but in a repeat of their previous engagement Darius managed to slip away, defeated but still alive to fight another day.

Alexander did not pursue Darius immediately, though. He had business in Babylon, the ancient capital of Mesopotamia. When Alexander arrived in this legendary metropolis he did not want to be perceived as a conqueror, and like so many other leaders before him and since, he sought to make the people of this ancient land in the Middle-East perceive him as their liberator rather than their conqueror.

Greatly aiding him in this was the governor of the city of Mazaeus, who guessing that the days of Persian dominion in Mesopotamia were over, sided with Alexander as long as Alexander allowed him to continue his leadership of the city. Alexander readily agreed, hoping that by installing a man who knew the language, culture and politics of the region would help to stave off any threat of insurgency.

With affairs in Babylon squared away, Alexander then led his men towards the ultimate goal of Persia itself. The main route inland was through a narrow high pass, surrounded by cliffs on all sides, known as the "Persian Gates". From Alexander's intelligence reports, he had ascertained that the local commander, Ariobarzaes, was lying in wait on the other side of this gateway with a considerable force of Persian soldiers.

They proved to be quite formidable, and as the daring Alexander and his Macedonian army attempted to charge through the pass they were cut down by a hail of arrows and stones. As the dead increased all around him Alexander realized he would not be able to make it through by direct assault. However, Alexander never lost his determination and it wasn't long before he found another way through the Persian Gates.

He was informed by a local shepherd that there was a narrow trail up the mountain that would serve as a shortcut through the gates. The only problem was the fact that the trail was so dangerously narrow that Alexander had to take hundreds of men and lead them single file, slowly and laboriously over this treacherous mountain pass. They eventually make it through to the great surprise of the Persians, attacking them from the rear while the rest of Alexander's forces crashed the gates from the other side.

After successfully dislodging Ariobarzaes and his militia, Alexander led his men to the city of Persepolis completely unopposed. After a brief occupation, Alexander then renewed his pursuit of Darius, but right in the middle of the chase he received word that a coup had occurred within the Persian ranks and that Darius himself had been removed from power, imprisoned by one of his own generals. Alexander was greatly frustrated by being unable to take down Darius himself.

He also had concerns that a renewed force of Persians with a new leader could lead a kind of guerilla warfare campaign against him almost indefinitely. Taking his fastest unit of cavalry, Alexander rushed to overtake the Persian caravan that held Darius hostage.

But even though he and his men raced across the landscape at top speed, the former emperor had already been stabbed to death by the time Alexander overtook the caravan. Without him or any of his men lifting a finger, Alexander realized that his arch-nemesis was no more.

Conclusion
Historical Autopsy

When Darius breathed his last, the reins of the great Persian Empire could be said to have officially passed to Alexander of Macedonia. In the days following the demise of Darius, Alexander's his men rolled through Persia like lightning, even cutting through swaths of northwestern India and making it the far eastern frontier of his empire. Although the span and width of his empire was expanding rapidly, his own personal lifespan would soon come to its end.

As fate would have it, the greatness of Alexander would only last for a very short time. Although the Macedonian king had survived vast armies of opposition and multitudes of risk and danger during his lifetime, it would be a night of raucous drinking that would bring him to his knees. He had been a hard drinker most of us life, but for some reason the booze hit him particularly hard on this night, with Alexander developing a high fever and dying shortly afterwards.

Some have suggested through the centuries that perhaps Alexander was poisoned, but since the ancient world did not readily provide the services of an autopsy, we will probably never know. Then again, through the shades of history, if we had to conduct an autopsy on the achievements of the young man from Macedonia named Alexander, only one pronouncement could be made: that he truly had been "Great".

Made in the USA
Monee, IL
25 January 2022

THE GREAT

What does it mean to be great? There have been many that have come through the sands of time proclaiming their own greatness. We see it in the news every day; leaders, heroes, tyrants, and even reality star presidential candidates claim that they are great. But what about Alexander the Great?

Inside you will read about...
✓ Alexander and the Happiness of Horses
✓ Aristotle and the First Day of School
✓ Philip's Family Drama
✓ Enemies and Friends
✓ The Real Battle Begins
✓ Changing Tides
✓ Signs and Wonders
✓ In Pursuit of Darius
✓ Historical Autopsy

The young man from Macedonia that took the world by storm creating one of the world's first major empires? He singlehandedly changed the course of history within a

MILFORD

Lost & Found

MICHAEL C. DOOLING